A Day in the Life of a...

Vet

Carol Watson

W

FRANKLIN WATTS

LONDON • NEW YORK • SYDNEY

This is Rosemary. She is a vet.
She treats sick or injured animals
in the country village where she lives.

Rosemary starts work at 9.00 am.
"Good morning, Betty," she says to
the receptionist. They talk over the
appointments for that day.

Betty takes down the details of the animals as they arrive at the surgery.
"This is Blossom," Charlotte tells Betty.
"She's cut her foot."

Clare and her sister have brought their tortoises for treatment. "This one's Toby, and that's Tommy," says Clare.
They all sit in the waiting room.

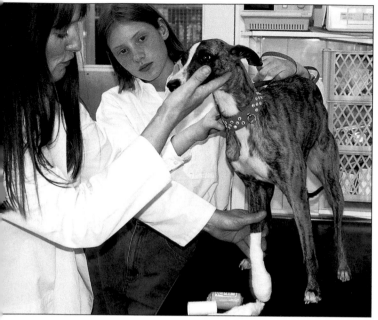

First Rosemary bathes and treats Blossom's foot. Then she wraps a bandage round it to keep out the dirt.

"This plastic collar will stop Blossom chewing off the bandage," she tells Charlotte.

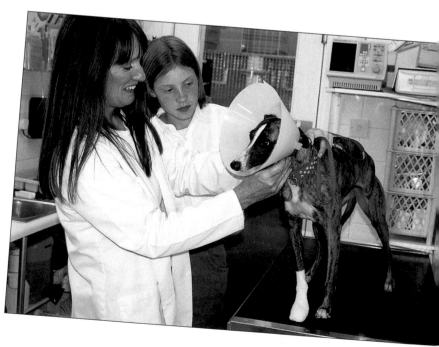

The tortoises are next. Rosemary weighs each one. "They both need worming," she tells the children. "The medicine goes down this tube. It doesn't hurt them."

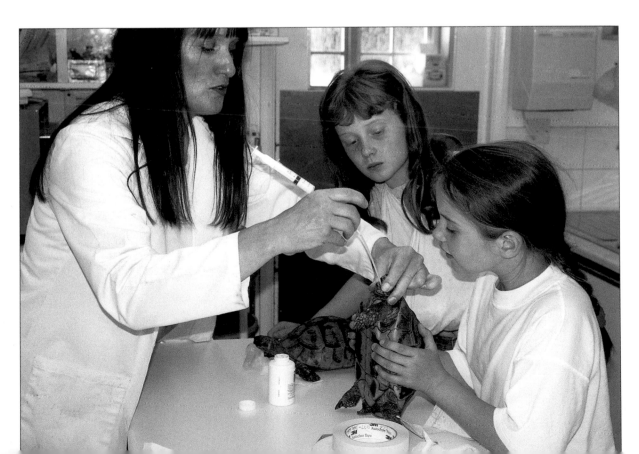

Meanwhile Rosemary's assistant, Mark, is checking over a dog called Lady.
"Her teeth and ears look fine," he tells her owner.

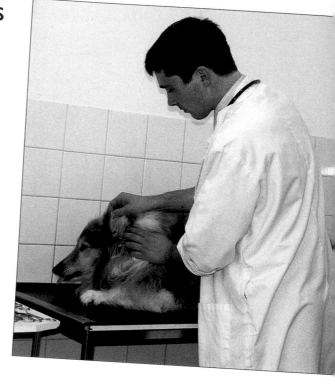

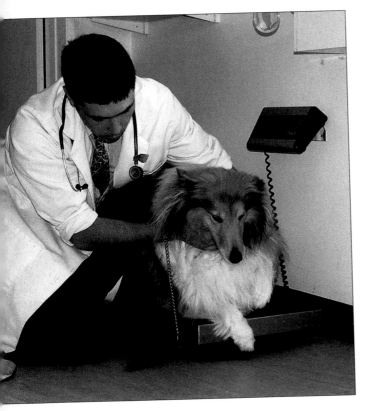

Lady lies on the scales. "She's a bit overweight," says Mark. "No more chocolates!"

Natalie's guinea pig, Pop, has caught
a cold. "I think she needs to be in a dry,
warm cage away from her sisters for
a while," Mark tells Natalie.

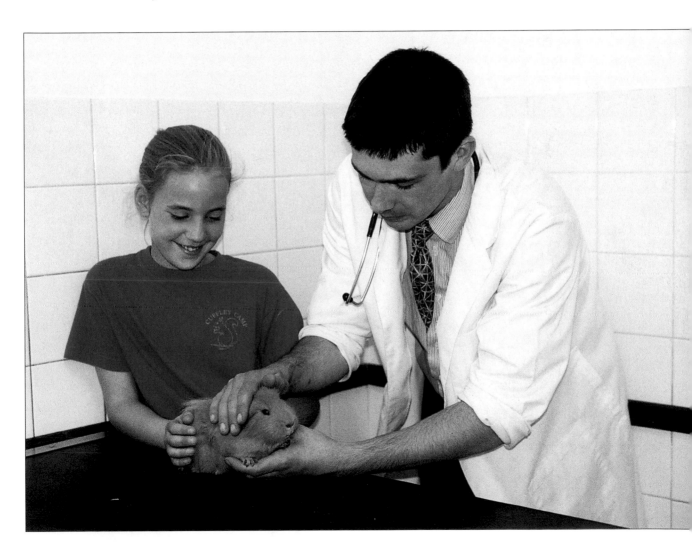

"Now it's time for Bertie's operation," Rosemary tells the veterinary nurse. "Let's get him ready."

First they get out the anaesthetic and other equipment they will need.

10

Then the vet
gives Bertie
an injection to
send him to sleep
for a while.

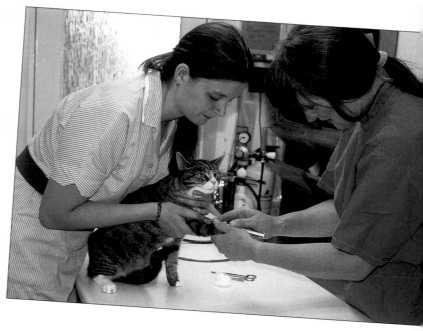

Before she
operates on the
cat, Rosemary
'scrubs up'
to stop germs
spreading.

Once the operation is over and Bertie is awake again, it is time for a home visit.

Rosemary takes her medical bag and special tool kit with her.

"Thanks for coming," says Robbie.
"My horse has gone lame."
Rosemary looks at the horse's hoof.

She uses a hoof knife to
clean out the foot.

"The foot is infected," Rosemary
tells Robbie. "I'll have to give her an
injection." The vet looks in her medical
bag for antibiotic medicine.

"I'll give her one shot now, and come
back to see her tomorrow," says Rosemary.
She tells Robbie to keep the horse's
foot clean.

On her way back,
Rosemary's mobile
phone rings.
"There's an emergency
call from Brook's Farm,"
Betty tells her.

John, the farmer,
greets the vet.
"There's a problem
with this ewe lamb,"
he tells her.
"She's coughing
and off her food."

16

The vet uses her stethoscope
to listen to the lamb's heart and lungs.
"She has a chest infection," says
Rosemary. "I'll give the animal
some medicine to help make it better."

Back at the surgery
Nick is waiting
with his cat.
"Pip is scratching a lot,"
he tells Rosemary.

"Your cat has fleas," says the vet.
"I'll give her a spray now, but
you'll need to do this again at home."

At last the calls are over for the day.
Rosemary reads her letters and
checks some information on the computer.
"Time to eat," she says to herself.

Animal First Aid

If you want to help your pets or small wild creatures that you find injured, here are some useful hints.

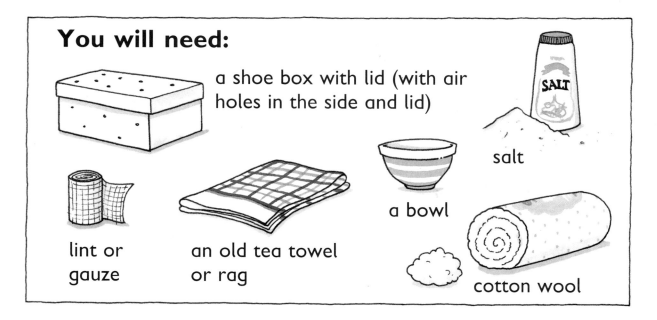

You will need:

a shoe box with lid (with air holes in the side and lid)

salt

lint or gauze

an old tea towel or rag

a bowl

cotton wool

Injured birds and other small wild creatures

1. If you find a baby animal make sure that the mother has gone for good. If the creature is not injured or in danger, leave it for a while and see if the mother comes back.

2. If the mother has gone, take an empty shoe box (with air holes) and put a warm, dry tea towel in it. Very gently lift the injured or abandoned animal into the box and put the lid on.

3. Put the box somewhere quiet and dark.

4. Ring the vet or RSPCA for advice on how to feed or treat it.

5. Return the creature to the wild when it is fit or old enough.

Other helpful tips

1. If your cat is sneezing or not eating, take it to the vet.

2. Treat a cut by cleaning it with warm, salty water.

3. If an animal is bleeding heavily, press a pad of lint or gauze firmly against the wound. Ring the vet immediately.

4. If your goldfish has spots, ask your vet about treatment for the water.

How you can help the vet help your pets

1. Check your cat or dog has been vaccinated against disease.

2. Protect cats and dogs against fleas and worms by using tablets or sprays regularly.

3. Always make sure your pets have good food, fresh water and clean bedding.

4. Make sure your pet gets plenty of exercise each day.

5. Warn your vet if you are taking an infectious animal to the surgery.

6. Never leave a dog inside a car without opening a window slightly.

7. Always make sure your pets are well looked after while you are on holiday.

Facts about vets

The word 'vet' is short for veterinary surgeon. There are different kinds of vet. Rosemary works in general practice. This means she treats and prevents disease in farm animals, household pets and horses in the area where she lives.

Other kinds of vets work in research and teaching, for the Ministry of Agriculture, Fisheries and Food (controlling epidemic diseases), in zoos, industry, public health service and overseas.

If you want to be a vet you will have to be prepared to deal with emergencies of any species of animal. This means you are obliged to treat an animal at any time, day or night, every day of the year.

To become a vet you need to spend at least five years at university and pass a veterinary science degree. Some vets then go on to specialise in one particular animal group, such as small animals and horses or farm animals.

Index

© 1997 Franklin Watts

Franklin Watts
96 Leonard Street
London
EC2A 4XD

Franklin Watts Australia
14 Mars Road
Lane Cove
NSW 2066

ISBN: 0 7496 2615 1 (hb)
      0 7496 3619 X (pb)

Dewey Decimal Classification
Number: 636.08

10 9 8 7 6 5 4 3 2 1

A CIP catalogue record for
this book is available from the
British Library.

Printed in Malaysia

Editor: Sarah Ridley
Designer: Kirstie Billingham
Photographer: Harry Cory-Wright
Illustrations: Ian McNee

With thanks to: Rosemary
Hobson and family, Nick and
Robbie Brown, Betty and John
Graves, Mark Pinches, Natalie Paul,
Lesley Fletcher, Louise Sharp and
'Lady'.